BASEBALL LEGENDS

Hank Aaron
Grover Cleveland Alexander
Ernie Banks
Johnny Bench
Yogi Berra
Roy Campanella
Roberto Clemente
Ty Cobb
Dizzy Dean
Joe DiMaggio
Bob Feller
Jimmie Foxx
Lou Gehrig
Bob Gibson
Rogers Hornsby
Walter Johnson
Sandy Koufax
Mickey Mantle
Christy Mathewson
Willie Mays
Stan Musial
Satchel Paige
Brooks Robinson
Frank Robinson
Jackie Robinson
Babe Ruth
Duke Snider
Warren Spahn
Willie Stargell
Honus Wagner
Ted Williams
Carl Yastrzemski
Cy Young

CHELSEA HOUSE PUBLISHERS

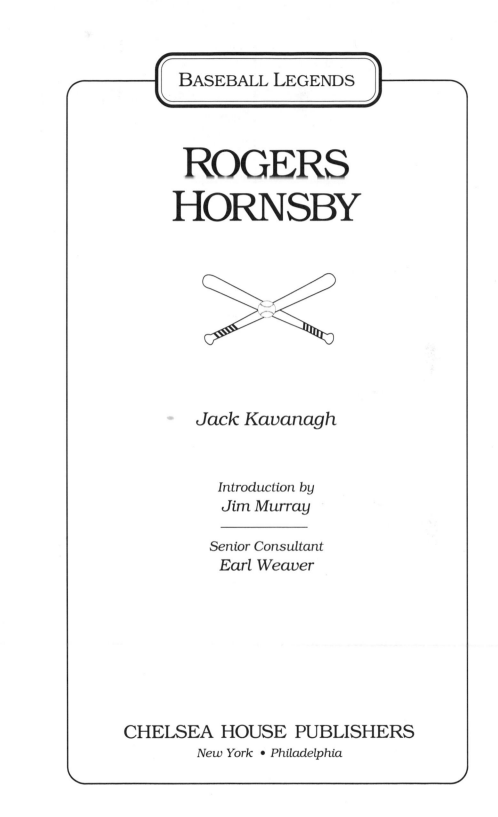

BASEBALL LEGENDS

ROGERS HORNSBY

Jack Kavanagh

Introduction by
Jim Murray

Senior Consultant
Earl Weaver

CHELSEA HOUSE PUBLISHERS
New York • Philadelphia

Produced by James Charlton Associates
New York, New York.

Designed by Hudson Studio
Ossining, New York.

Typesetting by LinoGraphics
New York, New York.

Picture research by Carolann Hawkins
Cover illustration by Dan O'Leary

First Printing

1 3 5 7 9 8 6 4 2

Library of Congress Cataloging-in-Publication Data

Kavanagh, Jack.
  Rogers Hornsby /Jack Kavanagh; introduction by Jim Murray;
senior consultant, Earl Weaver.
    p. cm.—(baseball legends)
  Includes bibliographical references and index.
  Summary: Follows the life and career of Baseball Hall of Fame
hitter Rogers Hornsby.
  ISBN 0-7910-1178-X.—ISBN 0-7910-1212-3 (pbk.)
  1. Hornsby, Rogers, 1896-1963—Juvenile literature. 2. Baseball
players—United States—Biography—Juvenile literature. 3. Hornsby
Rogers, 1896-1963. [1. Baseball players.] I. Title. II. Series.
GV865.H6K38 1991
92—dc20   90-41540
[796.357'092]   CIP
[B]   AC

CONTENTS

WHAT MAKES A STAR

Jim Murray

No one has ever been able to explain to me the mysterious alchemy that makes one man a .350 hitter and another player, more or less identical in physical makeup, hard put to hit .200. You look at an Al Kaline, who played with the Detroit Tigers from 1953 to 1974. He was pale, stringy, almost poetic-looking. He always seemed to be struggling against a bad case of mononucleosis. But with a bat in his hands, he was King Kong. During his career, he hit 399 home runs, rapped out 3,007 hits, and compiled a .297 batting average.

Form isn't the reason. The first time anybody saw Roberto Clemente step into the batter's box for the Pittsburgh Pirates, the best guess was that Clemente would be back in Double A ball in a week. He had one foot in the bucket and held his bat at an awkward angle—he looked as though he couldn't hit an outside pitch. A lot of other ballplayers may have had a better-looking stance. Yet they never led the National League in hitting in four different years, the way Clemente did.

Not every ballplayer is born with the ability to hit a curveball. Nor is exceptional hand-eye coordination the key to heavy hitting. Big-league locker rooms are filled with players who have all the attributes, save one: discipline. Every baseball man can tell you a story about a pitcher who throws a ball faster than anyone has ever seen but who has no control on or *off* the field.

The Hall of Fame is full of people who transformed themselves into great ballplayers by working at the sport, by studying the game, and making sacrifices. They're overachievers—and winners. If you want to find them, just watch the World Series. Or simply read about New York Yankee great Lou Gehrig; Ted Williams, "the Splendid Splinter" of the Boston Red Sox; or the Dodgers' strikeout king Sandy Koufax.

A pitcher *should* be able to win a lot of ballgames with a 98-miles-per-hour fastball. But what about the pitcher who wins 20 games a year with a fastball so slow that you can catch it with your teeth? Bob Feller of the Cleveland Indians got into the Hall of Fame with a blazing fastball that glowed in the dark. National League star Grover Cleveland Alexander got there with a pitch that took considerably longer to reach the plate; but when it did arrive, the pitch was exactly where Alexander wanted it to be—and the last place the batter expected it to be.

There are probably more players with exceptional ability who didn't make it to the major leagues than there are who did. A number of great hitters, bored with fielding practice, had to be dropped from their team because their home-run production didn't make up for their lapses in the field. And then there are players like Brooks Robinson of the Baltimore Orioles, who made himself into a human vacuum cleaner at third base because he knew that working hard to become an expert fielder would win him a job in the big leagues.

A star is not something that flashes through the sky. That's a comet. Or a meteor. A star is something you can steer ships by. It stays in place and gives off a steady glow; it is fixed, permanent. A star works at being a star.

And that's how you tell a star in baseball. He shows up night after night and takes pride in how brightly he shines. He's Willie Mays running so hard his hat keeps falling off; Ty Cobb sliding to stretch a single into a double; Lou Gehrig, after being fooled in his first two at-bats, belting the next pitch off the light tower because he's taken the time to study the pitcher. Stars never take themselves for granted. That's why they're stars.

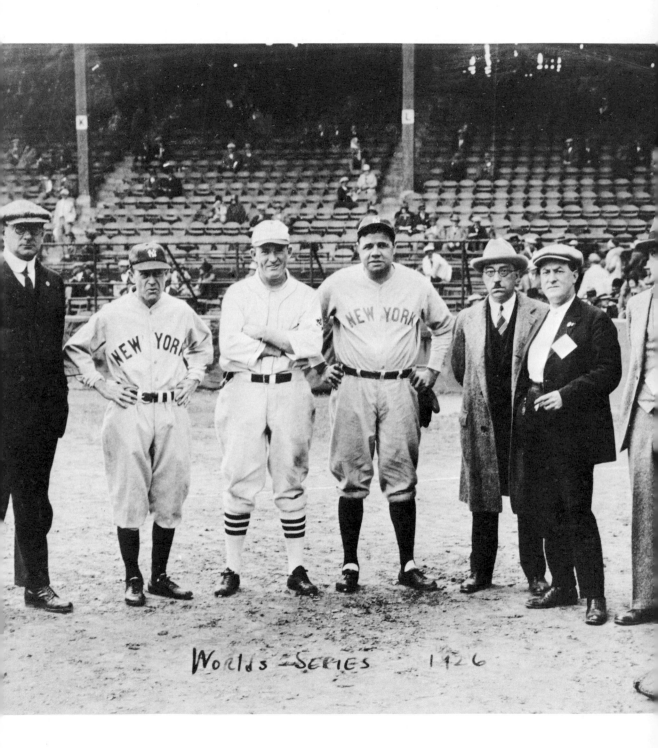

Worlds Series 1926

1

THE RAJAH AND THE SULTAN

The 1926 World Series between the New York Yankees and the St. Louis Cardinals brought together two of the finest hitters ever to swing at a baseball. The powerful Yankees were led by Babe Ruth, "the Sultan of Swat." The Babe's "royal rival" was the Cardinal's peerless hitter, Rogers Hornsby. Hornsby's name and imperial manner had led the newspaper writers to call him "The Rajah."

Hornsby was simply the best right-handed hitter the game has ever seen. Starting in 1920, he won six straight batting titles in the National League. No one has ever hit higher than his .424 in 1924. Only the legendary Ty Cobb has a higher lifetime average than Hornsby's .358, and only six players have a higher career slugging average than his .577.

In addition to playing second base in 1926,

The 1926 World Series pitted Hornsby's Cardinals against the powerful New York Yankees. Posing before game 1 are (left to right) sports writer Carl Brandebury, Yankee manager Miller Huggins, Hornsby, and Babe Ruth. Huggins was manager of the Cardinals when Hornsby was a rookie in 1915.

9

Hornsby was also the manager of the Cardinals, at 30 the youngest skipper in the league. Whether or not it was injuries or the stress of being the player-manager, his batting average slipped to .317 that year. Even so, he knocked in 93 runs and led the Redbirds to the National League pennant.

Heading into the 1926 World Series, the Cardinals were underdogs against the New Yorkers. But after six games the series was tied. The showdown in game 7 took place on October 10 under a gray sky at Yankee Stadium in New York City.

The Babe, who had hit three home runs in game 4 in St. Louis, homered in the third inning of the deciding game to put the Yankees ahead, 1–0. The Cardinals stormed back the next inning to take the lead, 3–1.

Then came the dramatic highlight of the final game. St. Louis was clinging to a 3–2 lead in the bottom of the seventh inning. The Yankees had the bases loaded with two out, and Tony Lazzeri, who had batted in more runs during the season than any other rookie, stepped to the plate.

Manager Hornsby risked everything by calling his tired veteran pitcher Grover Cleveland Alexander into the game. The day before, Old Pete, as he was often called, had evened the series at three games each with an easy, 10–2 victory. At 39, he had been considered washed up when he came to the Cardinals in mid-season. But Hornsby had used him in selected spots, and Alexander had made the difference in the pennant race, which the Cardinals won by just two games over Cincinnati.

Alexander had already beaten the Yankees twice in the World Series. He was thought to have finished his job. But in the seventh inning, Hornsby signaled to the bull pen for Alexander to face Tony Lazzeri. Old Pete threw only three warm up pitches

Hornsby takes batting practice during the 1926 World Series. Clyde Sukeforth, a player, manager and scout for more than 50 years, recalled Hornsby the hitter: "When Hornsby stepped into the cage to take batting practice before a game, everything on the field stopped. Everybody turned to watch him swing. And that included the old-timers, the tough old pros. Now that's an impressive tribute, I'd say."

and then ran the count to 1 and 2. His next pitch, a sharp-breaking curveball, struck out Lazzeri.

The game was not over, though. Hornsby asked Alexander to keep on firing. Alexander retired the Yankees in order in the eighth inning and set down the first two batters in the ninth inning. Then Babe Ruth stepped into the batter's box. With one swing he could tie the game.

The old pitcher cagily worked the corners of the plate while Ruth eyed each pitch closely. When the count reached three balls and two strikes, Alexander threw his favorite pitch. The ball shaved the corner of the plate, knee-high on the outside. Ruth did not swing at it, and the umpire, George Hildebrand, hesitated. Then he called, "Ball four." The Babe threw his bat aside and trotted to first base.

At second base, Hornsby, who rarely questioned an umpire's decision, kicked the bag. His action was more than a protest. It was also a signal to the team's rookie shortstop, Tommy Thevenow, that if there was a play at second base, Hornsby would handle it himself.

Bob Meusel, the American League home run leader the year before, was the next Yankee to bat, with the dangerous Lou Gehrig to follow. Ruth edged off first base. Alexander watched him closely. He did not want Ruth, still a fairly fast runner despite his size and increasing weight, to get too big a lead. The Yankees needed only to get Ruth home to tie the game.

Hornsby watched Bob O'Farrell, the Cardinals catcher, flash Alexander the signals. Then, out of the corner of his eye, Hornsby saw something he could scarcely believe. Ruth was attempting to steal second base.

As Hornsby remembered it: "Ruth went down on the first pitch just to make the surprise move as effective as possible, but O'Farrell's throw had him by 10 feet. He didn't say a word. He didn't even look around or up at me. He just picked himself off the ground and walked away to the dugout and I had lived through the greatest day any man could ask."

The play that ended the final game of the World Series was a routine one for the Rajah. But in fact he had barely made it through the World Series. He had an injured foot, a wrenched neck, and painful boils. Only sheer will power and pride kept him in the lineup. The fans who had cheered him as a player now praised him even more for his courage and leadership.

After their triumph, the jubilant Cardinals climbed aboard the Victory Special, the train that would take them back to St. Louis, where fans were already celebrating their first World Championship. The merry makers on the train paraded from car to car. But the door to the manager's compartment was closed. On the whole train, only the Rajah was quiet. The star player and manager of the World Series winner was preparing to leave the train before it got to St. Louis. Hornsby gave his reasons many years later: "I was always a hard-boiled guy who could keep his mind on the game no matter what. In the spring of 1926, the year we won it, we were playing a game in San Antonio and I visited my mother. She took me out on the porch, and you can call it mother's intuition or whatever you please, but she told me the Cards were going to win and that she would die on the day we clinched the pennant. And she said I should play the World Series before I came home to bury her.

"Well, on September 26, 1926, we beat the Giants in New York to clinch, and when I got back to the Alamac Hotel, there was a wire waiting for me. She was dead. We played and won the Series, and on the way back to St. Louis I changed trains and went home" to her funeral.

Rogers Hornsby was born on April 27, 1896, in Winters, Texas. He was Ed and Mary Hornsby's fifth child and the last of four boys. His unusual first name was actually his mother's maiden name.

Rogers's mother made his first baseball uniform, and his father bought him his first glove. While Mary Hornsby lived to see her son become baseball's greatest right-handed batter, his father did not. He died when Rogers was only four years old. On that fateful day, Rogers was outside the family ranch house in Winters, imitating how his older brothers played ball. All the Hornsbys were ballplayers; one of them, Everett (nicknamed Pep), even became a good pitcher in the Texas League.

Mary Hornsby rushed out of the house, gathered up her youngest son, and carried him inside. Rogers, still wearing his baseball glove, stood at his dying father's bedside. Eventually he was sent outside by his weeping mother. He went back to his game, too young to understand what was taking place.

"After the death of my father," Hornsby recalled, "We moved to my grandfather Rogers's farm near Austin. The older boys went to work to help support

Ft. Worth was a bustling Texas town when young Rogers was attending high school there.

the family, and after a few years, we moved to a house on the outskirts of Fort Worth. I was eight or nine then, and I knew I would become a ballplayer."

Rogers and his friends would often challenge boys from other neighborhoods to "get up a game." The kids would play as many as three games on Saturdays and Sundays. Rogers never ran out of energy, and he never tired of playing baseball.

Rogers got an after-school job in the meat-packing yards of Fort Worth when he was 12.

Around that time he began playing baseball against grown men, even though he weighed only 113 pounds. He usually played shortstop but would take any position that would get him into a game for any of the three stockyard teams that needed him.

Hornsby's boyhood idol was Ty Cobb, who was then a teenager with the Detroit Tigers. "He was my hero for years, even after I'd become a big league player myself," Hornsby said later. "I think he was the best all-around ballplayer the game has ever had."

At 14, Hornsby was still a tireless, skinny kid who played baseball from morning until night. He would rush out of high school as soon as classes ended and find a field where he and his friends played until it was too dark to see the ball.

"My mother was wonderful about understanding how much I wanted to be a ballplayer," he said. "She never nagged me about playing even when I'd come in long after meals were over. She never saw a game of professional baseball in her life, but she understood what the game meant to me."

When he was 15, Rogers played a season of football at Fort Worth's North Side High. He was the starting quarterback but quit the team to concentrate on baseball. Pep Hornsby, a spitball pitcher with Houston in the Texas League, kept an eye on his little brother. When Houston played against Fort Worth, he would get Rogers a job as the bat boy.

In 1914, when Rogers was 18, Pep took him to Dallas for a professional tryout. Rogers lasted just two weeks with the Fort Worth team before he was sent to Hugo, Oklahoma. He looked great in the field and was fast on the bases, but he was a weak hitter. He was soon sent to Denison, Texas, in the

Western Association. The man who would hit over .400 three times in the big leagues could only scratch out a .232 average as a rookie in the minors.

The next spring, a group of back-up players of the St. Louis Cardinals came to Denison for an exhibition game. The skinny shortstop who scooped up grounders like a major-leaguer quickly caught the attention of Cardinals head scout Bob Connery. In late August, Connery returned to Denison and bought Hornsby's contract for $500. Ironically, Connery had no idea he had discovered a future seven-time batting champ. The scout had signed the 19 year old for his fielding and speed.

Hornsby weighed only 135 pounds when he reported to Miller Huggins, the St. Louis manager. Because the young, 5-foot 11$\frac{1}{2}$-inch Texan looked so scrawny, Huggins instructed Hornsby to choke up on the bat. This was the way Huggins, who stood 5 inches shorter than Hornsby, had hit in his playing days.

On September 1, 1915, Rogers Hornsby made his first appearance as a big-leaguer. Hunched over the plate, he tried to get on with a walk but wound up tapping the ball weakly to the pitcher. It was an unimpressive debut, yet Huggins kept Hornsby in the lineup because he liked the slender teenager's hard-driving attitude. In 18 games, Hornsby hit a mere .246 with no home runs.

When the season ended, Huggins sat down with the young shortstop and told him, "You're a good ballplayer, son, but you're not big enough. I think we're going to have to farm you out."

Years later, after he had become a famous player, Hornsby liked to tell interviewers about this conversation. The naive youngster actually thought the Cardinals were going to send him to a farm somewhere, so he decided to get the jump on them. Instead of going home to Fort Worth, he spent the off-season on his uncle's farm in Lockhart, Texas. Rogers stuffed himself all winter with wholesome food and slept 12 to 14 hours a night. During the day he worked hard doing farm chores to build up his muscles. When he reported for spring training, Huggins was stunned to see Hornsby, who had previously weighed 135 pounds, now a solid 160-pounder.

"What happened to you?" the wide-eyed manager asked.

"I went to a farm, like you said," Hornsby replied. "I mean to stay with this ball club."

In the first pre-season game, Hornsby picked out the heaviest bat in the rack. He held it at the end of the handle, took the stance that would become his trademark, deep in the batter's box, and hit the first pitch for a triple off the center-field wall.

3

ON THE RISE

Hornsby was one of the better-fielding second basemen of his era. In four separate years (1917, 1920, 1922, and 1929), he led N.L. second sackers in one or more fielding categories.

The St. Louis Cardinals were a losing team when Rogers Hornsby joined them in 1915. They had been in the National League since 1892 and had never won a pennant. In fact, they had never even come close.

Hornsby was determined to change all that. From 1915 to 1918, he played mostly shortstop. In 1919, he played every infield position. From 1920 on, he was primarily a second baseman. Although he was one of the National League's best-fielding second basemen, it was his hitting that drew raves.

In 1916, Hornsby's first full season, he was fourth in the league with a .313 average. The next year he finished second with .327. After dropping to .281 in 1918, he again wound up second in the batting race, hitting .318 in 1919.

Major-league baseball changed dramatically the next year. There had been a big scandal in 1919 when eight players of the Chicago White Sox sold their services to gamblers and purposely lost the World Series. To give disillusioned baseball fans something new to cheer about the team owners decided to make baseball a more exciting game to watch. Pitches such as the spitball were outlawed, a livelier baseball was used, and a new ball was put into play every time one got stained or nicked. (A scuffed ball is harder to hit than a new ball because it moves and breaks more.) As a result, it was easier for the batters to get hits, and the number of runs scored per game increased dramatically. Babe Ruth, whom the Yankees had just acquired from the Boston Red Sox, stunned everyone by hitting a record 54 home runs in 1920. The old record, which Ruth had set the year before, had been 29 homers.

While Ruth was feasting on the pitchers in the American League, Rogers Hornsby was making hitting history in the National League. In 1920, he won the NL batting championship by hitting .370. And that was just the beginning. For the next five years, Hornsby's average would reach dizzying heights. He won six consecutive batting championships from 1920-1925 and hit over .400 a record-breaking three times.

Before Hornsby came along, the highest average in either league was .422. That record was set in 1901 by Hornsby's hero, Nap Lajoie. But in 1924, Hornsby hit .424, an average that still stands as the highest ever compiled in this century. For the years 1921 through 1925 Hornsby *averaged* over .400, the only player in major-league history ever to do this over five seasons. Even more impressive than Hornsby's batting average was his slugging percentage, the measure of a player's ability to hit for extra bases. During his career, Hornsby won an amazing number of batting titles, 7, but led in slugging average an even more impressive 9 times. Moreover, Hornsby was the home run champ in 1922 and 1925, when he cracked out 42 and 39, respectively.

While Babe Ruth was baseball's undisputed superstar, many fans could make a strong case that Rogers Hornsby was the more valuable of the two. In addition to his offensive power, he was a force to be reckoned with on defense. He led second basemen in the National League in fielding in 1922 and was an outstanding double-play man, using his strong arm to whip the ball to first base. Hornsby's manager in the early 1920s, Branch Rickey, judged Hornsby as the best second baseman of all at making the pivot on an infield double play. And Christy Mathewson, one of the greatest pitchers of all time, when rating players for a magazine article, called Hornsby the fastest runner in baseball.

Hornsby did have a weakness, however. He was not too sure on pop flies. This was easily explained by one reporter, who wrote, "The reason Mr. Hornsby is unfamiliar with pop ups is that he has hit so few of them himself." When Hornsby became player-manager of the Cardinals in 1925,

Straw-hatted St. Louis fans line up at Sportsman's Park to see Hornsby and the Cardinals. The old ballpark, expanded in 1925 to seat 30,000, was home to major-league baseball until 1966.

he would dictate coverage on pop flies. As he instructed shortstop Jimmy Cooney, "You take anything to my right and [first baseman Jim] Bottomley will handle anything on my left."

Just like when he was a boy, Hornsby had only one interest in life: playing baseball. As a major leaguer, he was totally dedicated to the game. He did not drink or smoke, and he got a lot of rest every night, usually sleeping 10 or more hours a night. He could sit and talk baseball for hours, particularly with veteran players and newsmen.

Hornsby was also a fanatic about keeping his vision sharp. To avoid eyestrain, he never read on a train and limited himself to reading only the baseball box scores anywhere else. Because he thought watching movies would tire the eyes, he never went to see them. His eyesight was too important to him.

The Hornsby eyes were alternately blue or hazel. "They change according to my mood," he once explained. They turned icy blue when anyone

"The Mahatma," Branch Rickey, was not much of a hitter, with a lifetime average of .239, or even much of manager— his teams never finished higher than fourth place. But as an executive, his innovative thinking brought the farm system and racial integration to baseball.

tried to take advantage of him, and they were a happy hazel when he watched a baseball coming up to the plate for him to bash.

One man who kept Hornsby's eyes blue for years was Sam Breadon. A prosperous automobile dealer, he became president of the Cardinals when the club was sold to a group of local businessmen in 1920. At first Breadon let field manager Branch Rickey handle all the team's business. Rickey, a college graduate, was a shrewd manipulator. However, Breadon eventually decided that the players were confused by Rickey's teaching methods and moved him into the front office. He replaced him in 1925 with Hornsby as manager. At the time, Breadon had no way of knowing whether Hornsby was a better manager, but he definitely was cheaper. Breadon would be paying Hornsby less to be both the second baseman and team manager than he had paid Hornsby and Rickey separately. Before long, however, Breadon would decide Hornsby had not been such a bargain after all.

4

HIGHS AND LOWS

When Hornsby replaced Branch Rickey as manager late in the 1925 season, the Cardinals were in last place. It was then that Branch Rickey, one of the smartest men in baseball history, made a big mistake. Although he was persuaded to stay on as general manager, Rickey sold his stock in the team to the new manager. The 1,165 shares Hornsby bought made him the club's second largest stockholder. Only Sam Breadon owned more. When the Cardinals became world champs the next year, the stock tripled in value.

In 1926 Hornsby had played the final season of a three-year contract which paid him $30,000 a year. His salary had not been increased when he became manager in 1925, but now he wanted a new multi-year contract. Money was not the main issue. His future as a player was in some doubt. While lesser players would have been more than happy with Hornsby's .317, it was a big comedown from his previous season's .403. And so were his 11 home runs compared to the league-leading 39 for 1925. In fact, only determination kept him in the lineup at all.

A foot injury early in the season had become a

Babe Ruth and Hornsby finished one-two in the 1920s in home runs, RBIs, and runs scored. Hornsby was the decade leader in hits with 2,085.

*Hornsby's 1933 Tatoo Orbit
Baseball Card.*

chronic disability that would cause him to miss many games in the future. Even more of a problem were the carbuncles, or boils, that broke out on his neck. Though it was agony at times for Hornsby to even put on his uniform, he never complained and managed to play 134 games at second base. Looking ahead, however, Hornsby was not sure how many playing days remained for him. He wanted the security of a long-term contract as manager.

But Sam Breadon was not happy with the man the entire city of St. Louis had come to idolize. Breadon seemed jealous of all the attention Hornsby was getting. As the principal owner, he thought he deserved more credit than the fans were willing to give to a businessman who had invested in a sports team. In addition, Breadon bitterly resented a quarrel with Hornsby that had taken place in front of the players.

The Cardinals were not a rich franchise. Even while they were contenders in the 1926 pennant race, there were plenty of empty seats at the games at Sportsman's Park. To make up for the club's low attendance, Breadon wanted the Cards to play exhibition games on their off days. It would be a smart business move. However, the fans in the minor-league cities they visited wanted to see the great Rajah play. Despite Hornsby's sore feet and boils, the tired arm he could not raise above his head, the grind of keeping track of two dozen players on the road, Breadon wanted baseball's greatest batter in the lineup. Hornsby disagreed.

As player-manager, Hornsby wanted to rest his players as much as himself. He worried particularly about 39-year-old Grover Cleveland Alexander, the Cardinals' all-star pitcher. Hornsby believed it was absurd to risk a chance to win the pennant and the money to be made from the World Series just to pick up small change playing exhibition games.

Tact was unknown to Rogers Hornsby. His dedication to plain talk and truth had earned him the nickname of "Mr. Blunt." In front of the players, the outspoken Hornsby told Sam Breadon exactly how he felt about the exhibition games, and then he threw the owner out of the clubhouse.

Rumors of trouble could soon be heard even over the fans' cheers. The angry Breadon was trying to force Hornsby to resign by withholding the three-year contract the manager was insisting on. Then, just five days before Christmas 1926, Breadon became the Scrooge of St. Louis by trading away the immensely popular Rogers Hornsby to the New York Giants for another future Hall of Fame second-baseman, Frank Frisch. In New York, the Giants veteran manager John McGraw became

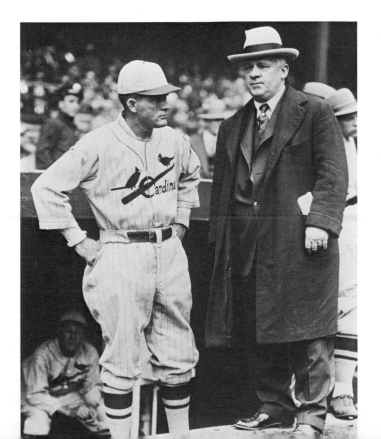

In 1926, Cardinals manager Hornsby chats with John McGraw, then in his 25th year of managing the Giants. McGraw was nicknamed "Little Napoleon" because of his abrasive, competitive style.

Hornsby (center) signs his contract in 1928 after being traded to Chicago. Cubs president Bill Veeck (left) and Cubs owner Phillip Wrigley look on.

Santa Claus to the local fans. He was giving them the greatest player in the National League.

Before Hornsby could even put on a Giant uniform, however, baseball rules required him to sell his stock in the Cardinals. Sam Breadon assumed that there would be no problem. He would gladly refund the money Hornsby had paid to Branch Rickey. But the stock had tripled in value, and Hornsby wanted what the stock was now worth. Hornsby claimed his success as manager had increased the value, and he should be the one to benefit from it. The argument dragged on through the spring.

As the two strong wills continued to clash, the season opener drew near. Baseball commissioner Judge Kenesaw Mountain Landis finally settled the dispute by convincing the owners of the other National League teams to make up the difference between the amount Hornsby wanted and the money that Breadon was willing to pay. Once that was resolved, Hornsby became a Giant.

Giants' manager John McGraw was very much

in need of Hornsby's services. Although he had won pennants with the Giants from 1921 through 1924, he had failed in 1925. And in the Cardinals' big year of 1926, his team fell into the second division. By 1927, McGraw was beginning to have some serious problems—both physical and financial—that interfered with his baseball responsibilities. And that was where Rogers Hornsby came in. McGraw asked Hornsby to run the team when he was not on hand.

What seemed like a fine solution to McGraw was viewed as another problem to some of the Giants players. Fred Lindstrom, a star third baseman, was especially resentful of Hornsby's managerial style. McGraw had instructed his infielders to always make sure that, with a man on first base, they got the force play even if the batter going to first was safe. But Hornsby wanted the ball fired to him at second as quickly as possible so he could try to complete the double play. When Hornsby criticized one of Lindstrom's double-play attempts for being too slow, the angry Giant complained, "I made it the way the Old Man wants us to make it."

"If that's the way the Old Man wants it," snapped Hornsby, "do it that way when he's in charge. When I'm in charge, do it my way." And when Lindstrom persisted with the argument, Hornsby flatly declared, "I'm not arguing with you, I'm telling you. You'll do as I say. And keep your mouth shut." Then he looked at the other Giants and told them, "And that goes for the rest of you." While Hornsby was merely trying to instill in his teammates the same kind of winning attitude he possessed, it did not make him very popular around the Giants dugout.

If the Giants disliked Hornsby as a manager,

they admired him as a player. Hornsby came through with a .361 average, 25 home runs, and 125 RBIs in 1927. So when McGraw traded Hornsby to the Boston Braves after the 1927 season for an overweight catcher, Shanty Hogan, and a second-string pitcher, Jimmy Welsh, the fans were dumb-founded. But once more, Hornsby's inability to get along with an owner—in this case, Charles Stoneham—had cost him a job.

It was a good deal for Boston. Determined to prove he was still the greatest hitter in the league, the Rajah won his seventh batting title in 1928, compiling a .387 average in spacious Braves Field, where the wind always seemed to blow against the batters.

Many years later, when Casey Stengel was managing the Boston Braves, one of his players was in a bad slump and blamed it on the ball park. "How can they expect anybody to hit up there? The wind is always with the pitcher. Nobody can hit up here."

"All I know," answered Stengel, "is that Hornsby played here one whole season and batted .387."

Hornsby was not only content with Braves Field, he was uncharacteristically fond of their owner, Judge Emil Fuchs. The combative second baseman might have happily spent the rest of his playing days in Boston if not for one thing: The Boston franchise was almost bankrupt. So when the Chicago Cubs made an irresistible offer to get him, Hornsby insisted that Fuchs accept. In addition to five players, the Cubs would pay the Braves $200,000—the most ever paid for a player at that time and enough to make the club solvent.

Hornsby packed his bags and moved his family, which included his wife, Jeannette, whom he had married in 1924, and two sons, Rogers, Jr., and

Bill, to Chicago for the 1929 season. Chicago eventually became Hornsby's permanent home. Although he would play for two more teams in the years ahead, he would always come back to the Windy City. Among the other attractions, the city had several racetracks, and Hornsby loved horse racing.

Hornsby's weakness for betting on the horses had already been used against him, mostly by Commissioner Landis, with whom he often clashed. One conflict arose when plans were being made for the 1926 World Series between the Cardinals and the Yankees. Landis, who ruled baseball with an iron hand, had definite ideas about how the teams would travel between New York and St. Louis. "I've selected the New York Central Railroad as the official route for the two clubs," he decreed.

"The Cardinals," Hornsby said, "will ride the

Hornsby with his wife, Jeannette, and William, one of his two sons, in the late 1920s. William briefly played minor-league baseball.

Hornsby strikes out in the 1929 World Series, one of a record eight times he fanned. This photo shows the classic Hornsby stance, with his right foot in the back corner of the batter's box, and the long diagonal stride forward.

Pennsylvania. We've used the Pennsylvania between St. Louis and New York for a long time, and I'm not going to take the business away from them now. Your job is to run the World Series and not to tell the ballplayers how to travel. If the Yankees want to take the New York Central, it's all right with me. We're taking the Pennsylvania."

On another occasion, Landis called upon Hornsby to defend himself against charges of betting on racehorses at the track, an activity that was not illegal. Hornsby was not about to apologize for his actions. "Playing the horses is my recreation," he told the commissioner, then added, "At least, if I lose, it's my own money."

As the 1929 baseball season began, Hornsby was looking forward to being just a player, not a player-manager, for the Cubs. He went to spring training at Catalina Island, off the California coast, as manager Joe McCarthy's most enthusiastic player. And as the regular season progressed, he carried the team along with him, hitting .380 and driving in 149 runs. Led by Hornsby and McCarthy, the Cubs went all the way to the World Series before bowing to the Philadelphia Athletics, 4 games to 1. Hornsby did not have a good series, knocking in just one run on five hits. He also struck out eight times in the five-game series, a world-series record, later tied by another Hall of Famer, Duke Snider.

Hornsby appeared in every game in 1929. Although he did not win the title, his overall play was good enough to earn him his second National League MVP award. The 1920s ended with Rogers Hornsby having averaged an incredible .382 for the decade. During the 10 years, he won seven batting titles. And still, he was bought—and sold— by four teams during the last four years.

It certainly was not his on-the-field actions that got Hornsby in trouble; it was his off-the-field words. Newspaper men knew Hornsby would answer all questions openly and honestly. He never claimed to have been misquoted and never spoke "off the record." However, his blunt honesty proved not to be his best policy.

5

PLAYER OR MANAGER

$\mathbf{I}$n 1930, Rogers Hornsby broke his ankle early in the season and played only 25 games at second base. Never again would he play more than 100 games in a season. And with that, his value to management as a superstar player dropped. From then on, he would be hired primarily as a manager. But while the Rajah's reputation as a legend seemed enough to convince owners that he would make a good manager, as soon as they hired him they rarely let him alone to do the job.

Hornsby was put in charge of the Cubs for the final weeks of 1930 and was player-manager again the following year. He was able to play in 100 games, and wound up with a more than respectable .331 batting average, 16 home runs, and 90 RBIs.

As a player, Hornsby came through on April 24, 1931, with three consecutive home runs against

On Memorial Day 1930, Hornsby (center) receives the 1929 Most Valuable Player Award from N.L. president John Heydler (left). Hornsby, on crutches because of a broken ankle sustained the day before, in a game in St. Louis, is the first N.L. player to win the award twice.

the Pirates at Pittsburgh's Forbes Field, clearing the fences in left, center, and right fields. As a manager, he never hesitated to put himself on the spot. The Cub fans were riding him one day as a game with the Boston Braves went into extra innings. In the top of the eleventh, Boston scored three runs, then the Cubs filled the bases with two out in their half. Hornsby, who was coaching at third, called time and put himself in to pinch-hit. The fans jeers turned to cheers as Hornsby delivered a bases-loaded home run to win the game.

Although the Cubs finished a disappointing fourth in 1931, Hornsby was optimistic about the 1932 season. He had added some solid new players, and owner Phil Wrigley seemed content to run his chewing gum empire and leave the baseball business to his manager. Unfortunately, Wrigley's general manager, a former sports writer named William Veeck, had other ideas. Veeck complained that Hornsby was rejecting all advice from the front office and that the players did not like their strong-willed manager. Veeck finally fired Hornsby in August and replaced him with Charley Grimm. Under Grimm, the Cubs came on strong to win the pennant and face the Yankees. As Hornsby later pointed out, that may have had less to do with the Cubs than with the team that had been in first place. The Pirates dropped 13 straight games in the stretch drive to lose out to their rivals from Chicago.

The Cub players confirmed their dislike of Hornsby by refusing him a share of their money from the upcoming World Series. The Cubs also voted only a partial share of the money to Mark Koenig, a former Yankee player who had played a major role in the Cubs pennant drive after joining the team at mid-season. This led to one of the most hostile meetings of two teams ever seen in a World

Series. The Yankees, led by Babe Ruth, came to town calling the Cubs cheapskates for their treatment of Hornsby and Koenig. To top it all off, the Yankees manager was none other than Joe McCarthy, who had been fired by the Cubs two years earlier. McCarthy wanted his share of vengeance, and he got it as the Yankees drubbed the Cubs in four straight games. The 1932 Series would best be remembered, however, for Babe Ruth signaling that he would hit a pitch over the center-field bleachers and then doing just that.

The following year, Hornsby's old team, the St. Louis Cardinals, invited him back. Branch Rickey, one of Rogers's best friends in baseball, was then riding high as the boss of the front-office, and even owner Sam Breadon did not object to having Hornsby back—but as a player, not a manager. Unfortunately, the Rajah was far from the player he had been. His right heel had developed a bone spur, and even surgery did not help. In fact, Hornsby later felt that he could have played a few more seasons if he had simply worn a rubber cushion in his shoe and had skipped the operation. Some years later Yankee slugger Joe DiMaggio had the same problem. Instead of following Hornsby's advice, DiMaggio let his doctors talk him into an operation that he also claimed shortened his career.

Despite his painful heel, Hornsby got into 46 games for the Cardinals in 1933 and batted a solid .325. In one stretch, he contributed a record-setting five straight hits as a pinch-hitter. One of these came in a highly dramatic game. Carl Hubbell of the Giants had pitched a 1-0 win in 18 innings against the Cardinals in the first game of a doubleheader. Young Roy Parmalee, a wild, hard-throwing Giant hurler, pitching in deepening twilight, was also working on a shutout in game 2. Yet Hornsby, after sitting on the bench all day long, lashed out a line-drive base hit when other batters were complaining it was too dark to play at all.

The Cards had won a pennant in 1928 while Rogers Hornsby was away, and in 1930 and 1931 manager Gabby Street had led the team to another pennant plus a World Series championship. However, the loss of the 1932 pennant to the Cubs and a drop to the second division early in 1933 was cause for concern. Before the 1933 ended, Street was replaced by the Cardinals' second baseman, Frank Frisch.

Hornsby was unavailable for the Cardinals' job because, at the suggestion of Branch Rickey, Hornsby was asked to manage the St. Louis Browns, the American League team that shared Sportsman's Park with the Cardinals. Other than Judge

Emil Fuchs, the owner of the Boston Braves, Hornsby had never met an owner he liked—until he joined the Browns and met Phil Ball. Although the Browns were a perennial second-division team, their owner was rich enough to support a losing club and optimistic enough to dream that he and Hornsby could turn things around. Ball was as plainspoken as the Rajah but wise enough to let his manager run the team. Hornsby had reason to believe that he had found the perfect place. But before the 1935 season even began, Phil Ball died suddenly.

After Ball's death, Hornsby continued to manage the team. The Browns struggled along in next-to-last place during 1935 and 1936 until the team was sold to Donald Barnes. That was when Hornsby's hobby of betting on racehorses got him into hot water again. In addition to his baseball interest, Barnes also owned a loan company. After buying some stock in the company, Hornsby used a certified check from his bookmaker to pay for the stock.

Once again, Hornsby was summoned to an owner's office. Barnes was unwilling to accept the check because it came from gambling. "There's nothing wrong with the money," Hornsby persisted, but Barnes refused, and soon Hornsby was out of a job. Hornsby had played very little in his years with the Browns, mostly pinch-hitting. In 1937—the last of his 23 big-league seasons—he left the team with a .321 average after appearing in only 20 games. He finished the season with the Denver Bay Refiners in the National Semipro Tournament, a comedown even from the lowly Browns.

6

BACK TO THE MINORS

Hornsby skippered a number of minor-league teams between 1938 and 1944. The first he managed was the 1938 Chattanooga Lookouts.

Though Rogers Hornsby was still a great celebrity in 1938, he could no longer get a job in the big leagues. But the Rajah was not worried. He had worked as an insurance salesman in St. Louis between seasons and had done quite well. He had many friends who were businessmen, and despite the hard times of the Great Depression, they could help him find work outside of baseball. Still, Hornsby was a baseball man. He had spent his life not only playing the game but studying everything about it. If there was no place for him in the big leagues, then the minors would have to do.

Hornsby went to spring training in 1938 as an instructor for the Minneapolis Millers of the American Association, then joined the Baltimore Orioles of the International League as a coach and pinch-hitter. By the end of June, he was managing the Chattanooga Lookouts of the Southern Association. In 1939, he managed Baltimore in the International League.

The 1940 season had already started when the Rajah was hired to manage the Oklahoma City team in the Texas League. After taking Oklahoma City to the final game of the playoffs, he returned in 1941 but resigned when the team ran out of money. In November, he signed a contract to become manager and general manager of the Fort Worth team. It was sort of a homecoming because he had grown up there.

Baseball continued into 1942, but there was a growing shortage of players as many of the nation's young men went into military service to fight in World War II. To make up for the thinning talent, Hornsby was now a 46-year-old pinch-hitter. The highlight of the year, however, was his election to the Baseball Hall of Fame. As unpopular as he was with the team owners, sportswriters had always appreciated Hornsby's willingness to talk baseball and his lack of hypocrisy. Of course, his records spoke for themselves. Only Ty Cobb's .367 lifetime batting average was higher than Hornsby's .358, and no right-handed batter even came close.

As a student of baseball, Hornsby was convinced his right-handedness had robbed him of a significant number of hits. "A left-handed batter starts two strides closer to first base and his momentum carries him toward the base when he swings," he commented. Although he envied left-handed batters for their automatic advantages, Hornsby had never even tried switch-hitting. And when he became a big-league batting instructor, he never attempted to change a right-handed batter to a left-handed one.

Ironically, at about the time he made the Hall of Fame, Hornsby once again found himself unemployed. He actually had to leave the country to find a job in 1944, instructing Mexican League

players and managing a team in Vera Cruz . It was a strange experience for Hornsby, who could not speak Spanish and thus failed to understand that the money man behind the Mexican League, Jorge Pasquel, did not always want the Vera Cruz team to win. Pasquel owned five different teams in the league, and he would move players from one to the other to build up fan interest. One day, Hornsby pinch-hit a game-winning home run in the ninth inning and learned he had found a new way to infuriate an owner. Pasquel had wanted Vera Cruz to lose the game and thereby extend a playoff series.

Hornsby gave up and went home to Chicago. In 1945, he became the director of the free baseball school sponsored by the Chicago *Daily News*. He did what he loved to do, touring the state of Illinois and teaching youngsters how to play the game.

When World War II ended, in 1945, there was

Hornsby displays his Hall of Fame plaque after being elected to the Hall of Fame in 1942.

an immediate boom in minor-league baseball the following year, with more leagues than ever before. But none of them offered the Rajah a job. Then, in 1947, he went to spring training as a batting coach for the Cleveland Indians. That was one role he really enjoyed, and he kept it through 1948.

In 1949, Hornsby found a place in a brand-new field: He became an announcer for the Chicago Cubs on WENR-TV. His only appearance in uniform that year was at an old-timers game at Wrigley Field.

Hornsby was at an age, 54, when most ex-players had already ended their careers in baseball. He had already achieved Hall of Fame status. He had an easy job that let him live at home with his family in financial security. Nevertheless, he felt most at home in a baseball uniform, and the 1950s found him back in the dugout.

When Hornsby was offered a chance to manage

Hornsby made Chicago his hometown and, in two stints in the 1940s and 1950s, he directed baseball programs for boys in the Windy City. Hornsby demonstrates the art of bunting while longtime Chicago mayor Richard Daley catches.

Beaumont in the Texas League, he could not resist. Although the team had finished the 1949 season in last place and was 19 games out of first on June 7, 1950, Hornsby drove his players all the way to the pennant. During the winter, he managed in Puerto Rico, then moved up to the AAA Pacific Coast League to manage the Seattle Rainiers in 1951. The Rainiers had been a second-division team the year before, but once more Hornsby turned his team around. This time they won the pennant and the championship playoffs.

The major leagues took notice, and suddenly Rogers Hornsby was in demand again.

7

THE RAJAH RETURNS

Back in 1932, the Rajah had been fired by Cubs manager William Veeck, Sr. It was Veeck's son Bill who brought Rogers Hornsby back to big-league baseball. When he was a youngster, Bill had helped around the team's office. One summer he helped plant the vines that have ever since covered the outfield wall at Wrigley Field. Later, after he was wounded as a marine during World War II and subsequently had a leg amputated, Bill Veeck became a baseball owner.

Veeck won a pennant at Cleveland in 1948. But by 1952 he was running the last-place St. Louis Browns. Because of the team's poor showing, he went to great lengths to draw crowds to the stadium. He had already startled the baseball world by sending a midget, Eddie Gaedel, to bat the year before. Now he astonished everyone by signing the no-nonsense Rogers Hornsby to a three-year-contract. Before signing, Hornsby made Veeck

"Mr. Blunt" was never gruff or surly with youngsters. While a batting coach for the Cubs in 1958, he chats with Deborah and Reed Landis, whose great-grandfather, Judge Landis, was commissioner of baseball.

promise not to embarrass him with wild stunts on the field. And Veeck did not. However, he made the same mistake as Hornsby's previous owners—trying to manage the team from the front office.

One day, the team was playing in Yankee Stadium in New York City and Veeck was listening to the game on a radio in his St. Louis office. Hornsby was coaching third base when a batter popped a foul near the field boxes. As fans stretched out their hands for the ball, umpire Joe Paparella thought one of them touched it and ruled interference, calling the batter out.

It was a controversial call, but Hornsby knew it was pointless to make an official protest over a matter that involved the judgment of an umpire. Protests are considered only when a rule may have been broken. Veeck sent a message ordering Hornsby to protest the game. The Rajah refused to do so. Not only would a protest fail to change anything, it went against Hornsby's reputation for getting along with umpires.

Hornsby had been thrown out of a game only once in his long career, and then he had been put right back in again. A young umpire had given Hornsby the thumb for protesting a fourth straight close call against him. But veteran umpire Bill Klem quickly overruled his colleague, explaining that Hornsby rarely complained and should be given the privilege of an honest difference of opinion. Another time, umpire Cy Pfirman failed to call a third strike against the Rajah, and the pitcher, a mountain of a man called Jumbo Jim Elliott, shouted a complaint.

Pfirman then walked toward the pitcher and quietly explained things to him. "Whenever it's a strike," the ump said, "Mr. Hornsby will let you know about it."

Elliott was so mad that he burned the next pitch over the middle of the plate with every ounce of his strength. And Hornsby proceeded to smash it over the fence for a home run.

Clearly, Hornsby was not one to argue with umpires.

The day after the incident at Yankee Stadium, Veeck met Hornsby at the Kenmore Hotel in Boston, where the Browns' next game would be played. Veeck now realized he had made a mistake in hiring the strong-willed Hornsby and was looking to pay off the remainder of the three-year-contract, even though Hornsby had only worked half a season. Once again, the players were in revolt against the hard taskmaster. Veteran pitcher Satchel Paige, whose real age was a mystery although he was at least 45, later said, "Hornsby and me were from different schools. He ran his ball

Rogers Hornsby and Bill Veeck, Jr., just after Hornsby was hired to manage the Browns in 1952. Veeck was part-owner of the Indians in 1948, then sold them and bought the Browns, and twice later bought and sold the White Sox.

Rogers Hornsby (number 42) watches the play that will lead to his being fired as Browns manager. Yankee Gil McDougald tries unsuccessfully to catch a foul pop (arrow indicates ball). While the ball was in fair territory, a fan touched it, and the umpire ruled the Browns batter out for interference. Veeck, listening to the game on the radio, called Hornsby and ordered him to protest the call, an order which Hornsby refused.

club just like an army. He was one of those run-run-run men. We were all lined up out there on the field, and Hornsby came marching past all of us, asking how old we were.

"'I'm sixty-one,' I told him, kind of kidding. You don't kid Hornsby.

"He asked the kid standing next to me how old he was, and the kid told him seventeen, real truthful-like. Then Hornsby turned back to me and told me to do the same things the kid of seventeen was doing, running around the field, chasing flies, grabbing grounders, and then running around the field about four more times.

"'Mr. Hornsby,' I said, 'tell me, are you trainin' Ol' Satch for relief pitchin' or for the army?'"

But Paige, who in 1952 was 12–10 for the seventh-place Browns, grudgingly gave Hornsby some of the credit. "Maybe all that work helped," the great pitcher admitted. "I got tangled up in some ball games that'd have killed me if I hadn't been in the shape I was."

So Hornsby packed his bags, fired just 51 games into the season by Bill Veeck, Jr., just as he had been fired by Veeck, Sr., 20 years earlier. When the younger Veeck hired Hornsby in 1952 the owner's mother wrote to him, "What makes you think you're smarter than your daddy was?" Less than two months later, when Veeck fired Hornsby, she wrote again: "What did I tell you?"

Hornsby could have taken it easy after leaving the Browns. He did not need to work because the team would keep sending him paychecks for a long time. Actually, the Rajah had settled for less money than he was entitled to. It was a gracious gesture he might not have made had he known Bill Veeck was going to accept a plaque from the players thanking him for "the greatest act to end slavery since the Emancipation Proclamation." There was even some suspicion, but no proof, that the promotion-minded Veeck had the plaque made up himself and then urged the players to make the presentation.

But Hornsby was soon back at work, this time managing the Cincinnati Reds. Midway through the 1952 season he took over the last-place Reds and got them up to sixth place. But when he failed to get them out of the second division the following year, he was fired again just 8 games before the end of the 1953 season. It was the sixth and last major-league team the Hall of Famer would manage.

Hornsby settled down to domestic life in Chicago. He was named director of Mayor Richard Daley's Youth Foundation Recreation Program, teaching baseball to youngsters. He loved the work, continuing it until 1957. Then, because he was a man who could not get big-league baseball out of his system, he accepted a full-time job as batting coach for the Chicago Cubs. His main assignment was to help develop shortstop Ernie Banks as a hitter—and that is exactly what he did. Banks, who had never batted over .300, had back-to-back .300-plus seasons, hit 92 home runs in two years, and led the league in RBIs both seasons Hornsby coached him. Thanks in large part to Hornsby, Banks was the National League MVP for 1957 and 1958, even though the Cubs finished far down in the standings.

The Rajah continued as batting coach in 1959. It was pleasant work for a man in his sixties. He lived within walking distance of Wrigley Field. There were no night games to disturb his routine, and he had a great relationship with the Cubs manager, Bob Scheffing. But before Hornsby could get too comfortable, the Cubs fired Scheffing and brought back Charley Grimm, the man who had replaced Hornsby as the Cubs' manager in 1932. Now, almost thirty years later, Grimm, an old antagonist of Hornsby's, announced that he did not need a batting coach for 1960. Hornsby returned to the minors as a farm team instructor. Grimm lasted just 16 games as manager of the Cubs before being replaced by Lou Boudreau.

The retirement age of 65 arrived for Rogers Hornsby in 1961. Lucky for him, two other old-timers who still felt they had something to contribute to the game were then in the process of taking control of the brand-new New York franchise, the Mets. Casey Stengel, who had been discarded by the New York Yankees at age 71, was

Hornsby managed the Cincinnati Reds in 1952 and 1953. Before a 1953 Reds spring training game, he gives some batting tips to Dodgers first baseman Gil Hodges.

With more than 100 years of baseball experience between them, Casey Stengel and Rogers Hornsby contemplate the chances of one of baseball's two newest teams, the 1962 Mets.

the team's manager. After winning the pennant in 1960, his tenth in 12 years with the Yankees, Stengel and general manager George Weiss, also over 70, had been told by the Yankee owners they were too old to stay with the team. To Weiss and Stengel, Hornsby seemed like a youngster.

Because the Mets would not begin playing until 1962, they made Rogers Hornsby a scout for 1961. The new Mets would be drafted or bought from other teams. Stengel and Weiss wanted the knowledgeable Hornsby to watch the teams of both leagues as they passed through Chicago, playing the Cubs at Wrigley Field or the White Sox at Comiskey Park, and evaluate the players.

When the New York Mets went to spring training for the first time in 1962, Rogers Hornsby went with them as batting coach. The new team struggled through its first season, winning only 40 games while losing 120 and finishing in last place, 19 games behind ninth-place Chicago. But for Rogers Hornsby it was a last hurrah, a final time to put on a major-league uniform and be part of a team. At the end of the season, Hornsby went back to Chicago, but Stengel and Weiss expected him back in 1963. Much work would have to be done to create the Miracle Mets who would surprisingly win the World Series six years later.

However, the Mets would have to succeed without further help from Rogers Hornsby. On January 5, 1963, he checked into Wesley Memorial Hospital in Chicago. Of all things, the man who had protected his eyes by avoiding movies and limiting his reading had developed cataracts, an eye condition that blurs the vision and can lead to blindness. Coincidentally, another famous ex-ballplayer, Ted Lyons, a Hall of Fame pitcher from the Chicago White Sox, had the very same problem. The two old-timers went in the hospital together, taking rooms across from each other, but only Lyons went home. Hornsby died of a heart attack following an operation to remove the cataracts. The greatest right-hand hitter in baseball history was buried a few days later in Hornsby Bend, Texas.

CHRONOLOGY

Apr. 27, 1896	Born Rogers Hornsby in Winters, Texas
Sept. 10, 1915	Makes major-league debut with St. Louis Cardinals
1920	Wins first of six consecutive batting titles
1922	Hits over .400 for first time; sets NL home-run record (42)
1924	Bats .424, highest average in 20th-century major-league baseball
1925	Bats .403 as player-manager of St. Louis Cardinals; wins NL MVP Award
1926	Leads Cardinals to their first pennant and World Series victory
Dec. 20, 1926	Traded to New York Giants
Jan. 10, 1928	Traded to Boston Braves
1928	Wins seventh NL batting title
Nov.7, 1928	Traded to Chicago Cubs
1929	Wins second NL MVP Award; Cubs win pennant
Sept. 23, 1930	Named manager of Chicago Cubs
Aug. 2, 1932	Fired as manager of Cubs
Oct. 24, 1932	Signs as player with St. Louis Cardinals
July 27, 1933	Named manager of St. Louis Browns
July 23, 1937	Fired by the Browns
1938-1944	Manages several minor-league teams
1945-1948	Directs Chicago *Daily News* baseball school for boys
1949	Becomes TV announcer for Chicago Cubs games
1952	Hired—then fired—as manager of St. Louis Browns
Aug. 1, 1952	Hired as manager of Cincinnati Reds
Sept. 17, 1953	Fired by Reds
1957-59	Coaches for the Chicago Cubs
1961	Scouts for the New York Mets
1962	Serves as batting coach for Mets
Jan.5, 1963	Dies of a heart attack in Chicago, Illinois

ROGERS HORNSBY

NATIONAL LEAGUE BATTING CHAMPION
7 YEARS - 1920 TO 1925; 1928. LIFETIME
BATTING AVERAGE .358 HIGHEST IN
NATIONAL LEAGUE HISTORY. HIT .424 IN
1924, 20TH CENTURY MAJOR LEAGUE RECORD.
MANAGER 1926 WORLD CHAMPION ST. LOUIS
CARDINALS. MOST-VALUABLE-PLAYER
1925 AND 1929.

MAJOR LEAGUE STATISTICS

St. Louis Cardinals, New York Giants, Boston Braves, Chicago Cubs, St. Louis Browns

YEAR	TEAM	G	AB	R	H	2B	3B	HR	RBI	BA	SB
1915	STL N	18	57	5	14	2	0	0	4	.246	0
1916		139	495	63	155	17	15	6	65	.313	17
1917		145	523	86	171	24	17	8	66	.327	17
1918		115	416	51	117	19	11	5	60	.281	8
1919		138	512	68	163	15	9	8	71	.318	17
1920		179	589	96	218	44	20	9	94	.370	12
1921		154	592	131	235	44	18	21	126	.397	13
1922		154	623	141	250	46	14	42	152	.401	17
1923		107	424	89	163	32	10	17	83	.384	3
1924		143	536	121	227	43	14	25	94	.424	5
1925		138	504	133	203	41	10	39	143	.403	5
1926		134	527	96	167	34	5	11	93	.317	3
1927	NY N	155	568	133	205	32	9	26	125	.361	9
1928	BOS N	140	486	99	188	42	7	21	94	.384	5
1929	CHI N	156	602	156	229	47	8	39	149	.380	2
1930		42	104	15	32	5	1	2	18	.308	0
1931		100	357	64	118	37	1	16	90	.331	1
1932		19	58	10	13	2	0	1	7	.224	0
1933	2 teams	STL N	(46 G—.325)		STL A	(11 G—.333)					
	total	57	92	11	30	7	0	3	23	.326	1
1934	STL A	24	23	2	7	2	0	1	11	.304	0
1935		10	24	1	5	3	0	0	3	.208	0
1936		2	5	1	2	0	0	0	2	.400	0
1937		20	56	7	18	3	0	1	11	.321	0
Totals		2259	8173	1579	2930	541	169	301	1584	.358	135
World Series (2 years)		12	49	6	12	2	1	0	5	.245	1

FURTHER READING

Allen, Lee and Tom Meany. *Kings of the Diamond.* New York: G.P. Putnam, 1965.

Broeg, Bob. *Super Stars of Baseball.* St. Louis, MO: The Sporting News, 1971.

Carmichael, John. *My Greatest Day In Baseball.* New York: A.S. Barnes, 1950.

Stockton, J. Roy. *Rogers Hornsby.* New York: David McKay, 1953.

Hornsby, Rogers and Bill Surface. *My War With Baseball.* New York: Coward-McCann, 1962.

Meany, Tom. *Baseball's Greatest Hitters.* New York: A.S. Barnes, 1950.

Meany, Tom and Tommy Holmes. *Baseball's Best.* New York: Franklin Watts, 1964.

Okrent, Dan and Steve Wulf. *Baseball Anecdotes.* New York: Oxford University, 1989.

Seaver, Tom. *How I Would Pitch to Babe Ruth.* Chicago, IL: Playboy Press, 1974.

Shatzkin, Mike. *The Ball Players.* New York: William Morrow, 1990.

Thorn, John. *Total Baseball.* New York: Warner, 1989.

Williams, Joe. *The Joe Williams Baseball Reader.* Chapel Hill, NC: Algonquin, 1989.

INDEX

PICTURE CREDITS
AP/Wide World: pp. 8, 30, 33, 34, 36, 39, 46, 48, 55; From the collection of Jack Kavanagh, p. 28; National Baseball Library, Cooperstown, NY: pp. 2, 11, 23, 24, 26, 29, 42, 45, 51, 52, 56, 58, 60; The Sporting News: p. 20; UPI/Bettmann: pp. 11, 16

JACK KAVANAGH, a free-lance writer of sports stories, began writing about sports as a high school correspondent for the *Brooklyn Eagle* in the 1930s. He has been a contributing editor to *Sports History* and his writing has appeared in various magazines, including *Sports Heritage*, *Vine Line* and *Diversions*. His work is included in *The Ball Players*, *Total Baseball* and other baseball anthologies. Mr. Kavanagh lives in North Kingston, Rhode Island.

JIM MURRAY, veteran sports columnist of the *Los Angeles Times*, is one of America's most acclaimed writers. He has been named "America's Best Sportswriter" by the National Association of Sportscasters and Sportswriters 14 times, was awarded the Red Smith Award, and was twice winner of the National Headliner Award. In addition, he was awarded the J. G. Taylor Spink Award in 1987 for "meritorious contributions to baseball writing." With this award came his 1988 induction into the National Baseball Hall of Fame in Cooperstown, New York.

EARL WEAVER is the winningest manager in Baltimore Orioles history by a wide margin. He compiled 1,480 victories in his 17 years at the helm. After managing eight different minor league teams, he was given the chance to lead the Orioles in 1968. Under his leadership the Orioles finished lower than second place in the American League East only four times in 17 years. One of only 12 managers in big league history to have managed in four or more World Series, Earl was named Manager of the Year in 1979. The popular Weaver had his number 5 retired in 1982, joining Brooks Robinson, Frank Robinson, and Jim Palmer, whose numbers were retired previously. Earl Weaver continues his association with the professional baseball scene by writing, broadcasting, and coaching.